D1200408

Leadership Skills & Character Building

SELF-CONFIDENCE

TITLES IN THE SERIES

- Communication Skills
- Initiative, Grit & Perseverance
- Integrity & Honesty
- Organization & Problem-Solving
- Self-Confidence
- Self-Discipline & Responsibility
- Tolerance & Cooperation

Leadership Skills & Character Building

SELF-CONFIDENCE

Sarah Smith

MASON CREST

Mason Crest
450 Parkway Drive, Suite D
Broomall, Pennsylvania PA 19008
(866) MCP-BOOK (toll free)

First printing
9 8 7 6 5 4 3 2 1

ISBN: 978-1-4222-3999-5
Series ISBN: 978-1-4222-3994-0
ebook ISBN: 978-1-4222-7790-4

Cataloging-in-Publication Data on file with the Library of Congress.

Printed and bound in the United States of America.

QR CODES AND LINKS TO THIRD-PARTY CONTENT

You may gain access to certain third-party content ("Third- Party Sites") by scanning and using the QR Codes that appear in this publication (the "QR Codes"). We do not operate or control in any respect any information, products, or services on such Third-Party Sites linked to by us via the QR Codes included in this publication, and we assume no responsibility for any materials you may access using the QR Codes. Your use of the QR Codes may be subject to terms, limitations, or restrictions set forth in the applicable terms of use or otherwise established by the owners of the Third-Party Sites. Our linking to such Third-Party Sites via the QR Codes does not imply an endorsement or sponsorship of such Third-Party Sites or the information, products, or services offered on or through the Third-Party Sites, nor does it imply an endorsement or sponsorship of this publication by the owners of such Third-Party Sites.

Contents

KEY ICONS TO LOOK FOR:

Words to Understand: These words with their easy-to-understand definitions will increase the reader's understanding of the text while building vocabulary skills.

Sidebars: This boxed material within the main text allows readers to build knowledge, gain insights, explore possibilities, and broaden their perspectives by weaving together additional information to provide realistic and holistic perspectives.

Educational Videos: Readers can view videos by scanning our QR codes, providing them with additional content to supplement the text. Examples include news coverage, moments in history, speeches, iconic sports moments, and much more!

Text-Dependent Questions: These questions send the reader back to the text for more careful attention to the evidence presented there.

Research Projects: Readers are pointed toward areas of further inquiry connected to each chapter. Suggestions are provided for projects that encourage deeper research and analysis.

Series Glossary of Key Terms: This back-of-the-book glossary contains terminology used throughout the series. Words found here increase the reader's ability to read and comprehend higher-level books and articles in this field.

INTRODUCTION: INSPIRATION TO THE READER

The most effective leaders have a combination of intellectual intelligence (IQ), technical skills, and emotional intelligence (EI). Emotional intelligence is an essential ingredient. EI is the act of knowing, understanding, and responding to emotions, overcoming stress in the moment, and being aware of how your words and actions affect others. Emotional intelligence consists of five attributes: self-awareness, self-management, empathy, motivation, and effective communication.

The Unrelenting Athlete

"I've missed more than 9000 shots in my career. I've lost almost 300 games. Twenty-six times I've been trusted to take the game winning shot and missed. I've failed over and over and over again in my life. And that is why I succeed."

–Michael Jordan

The Bold Poets

"I've learned that people will forget what you said, people will forget what you did, but people will never forget how you made them feel."

–Maya Angelou

"What's money? A man is a success if he gets up in the morning and goes to bed at night and in between does what he wants to do."

–Bob Dylan

Becoming more confident as a leader in any capacity will help you inspire others and set a positive example. Gaining confidence in yourself, and finding more joy and peace of mind as you go about life, will help you handle all the successes, challenges, and setbacks along the way. Inside the pages of this book we will discuss all the components to improving your leadership skills, bringing you more confidence and building your character to become the leader you want to be some day.

The Inspiring Creators

"Whether you think you can or you think you can't, you're right."
—Henry Ford

"Strive not to be a success, but rather to be of value."
—Albert Einstein

The Captivating Writer

"Twenty years from now you will be more disappointed by the things that you didn't do than by the ones you did do, so throw off the bowlines, sail away from safe harbor, catch the trade winds in your sails. Explore. Dream. Discover."
—Mark Twain

Words to Understand

collaborate: to work with another person or group in order to achieve or do something

innovations: new ideas, methods, or devices

inspire: to move (someone) to act, create, or feel emotions

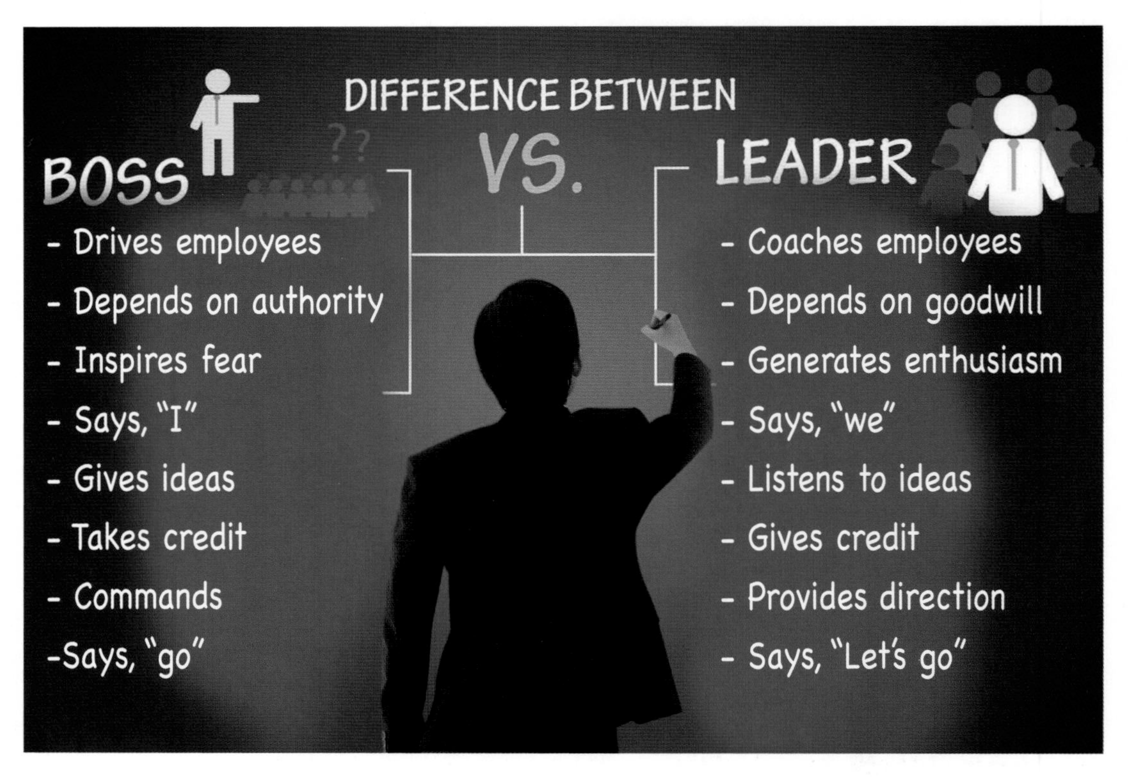

This illustration describes the differences between a bad boss and a good leader. A good leader will inspire and motivate others, whereas a bad boss will cause disharmony and unhappiness.

Chapter One
HOW SELF-CONFIDENCE CAN BUILD CHARACTER & LEADERSHIPS SKILLS

Now more than ever, the world needs effective leaders. Why? Because on local, national, and international scales, change is happening rapidly. In areas ranging from technology to the environment, politics to human rights, health care to space travel, there are new advances, **innovations**, and challenges happening at a faster pace than ever before in history. In order to navigate this change and create a more sustainable and healthier planet for current and future generations, the world needs people who can **inspire**, **collaborate**, innovate, and ultimately bring people together in harmony.

But while leadership is an important skill, it's not often explicitly taught in academic settings. Today's youth could benefit from learning how to recognize and develop the traits of quality leadership—traits like fairness, generosity, kindheartedness, tact, and integrity.

Of course, of all the traits that effective leaders have, confidence may be one of the most crucial. After all, setbacks and failure are a given in life, so a leader's ability to face, learn from, and rise above these challenges—which is what confidence allows one to do—can drastically influence whether or not a leader will be successful.

The key here is *confidence,* which is different than cockiness. It's about certainty, which is different than selfishness. It's about self-belief—which is much different from self-delusion, denial, or bragging. These subtle differences, along with other related concepts, will be discussed in greater detail in this book.

People with self-confidence are those who can accept themselves for who they are—"flaws" and all. It is important, therefore, that those who lack self-confidence should learn how to become more positive about themselves.

What to Expect From This Book

In this book, students will be taken on an inspiring journey in self-discovery, self-confidence, and self-love. While these subjects may seem trite or clichéd, the reader is encouraged to think about them as valuable assets they can develop and grow for the betterment of themselves and their world. Having such self-affirming beliefs will help teens and young adults achieve in virtually every facet of life: academics, vocations, relationships, physical health, and even finances and creativity.

The first topic to be covered will be the idea of self-love. Perhaps the greatest challenge that people face when struggling with confidence is the idea of loving and accepting themselves for who they are. Learning to like and even celebrate oneself—"flaws" and all—is a crucial, lifelong lesson in building confidence and leadership ability.

Next, the focus shifts from learning how to like oneself to learning how to like, get along with, and ultimately make friends with other people. The world shines brightly on folks who can bring others together and who see the common humanity between all the different races, cultures, ethnicities, genders, religions, sexual orientations, and so on. It's these people who connect and make friends easily (and who themselves prove to be good friends) who often have greater opportunities for success. In short: confidence leads to connection, and vice versa.

Of all the areas in life in which people struggle to feel confident in (especially in the case of adolescents, teens, and young adults), body image is one of the most significant. How a person feels about they way they look will have great influence on not only the way they carry themselves in public but also on how they treat their body, how they interact with others, and how they feel about themselves as worthy people. The chapter on body image will give readers some powerful insights that can help them learn to be more confident and caring about their bodies, even as they change.

As mentioned earlier, confidence in oneself and one's abilities is almost never more important than when dealing with challenges, setbacks, failures, and mistakes. This chapter will provide exercises, ideas, and approaches intended to help students learn how to deal with (though not necessarily avoid) their mistakes in a more productive and self-affirming way.

Related to this topic is the broad issue of negativity: negativity within oneself and from the external world (other people, the media, etc.). For better or worse, positivity *and* negativity are a natural part of life, and everyone experiences highs and lows and ups and downs. The next chapter discusses the issue of negativity and how young people can deal with it in new ways (and perhaps even use it to their advantage).

Lastly, readers of this book will be tasked with the one lifelong challenge that has tripped up people from all walks of life: being authentic. It's reasonable to suggest that much of the strife, conflict, and drama in this world comes from inner turmoil—from the stress of not being true to oneself and failing to practice that age-old wisdom: "Be yourself." What does being yourself even mean? And how does one do this? These questions and more will be discussed in the final chapter.

Poverty to Wealth: Malala Yousafzai

Malala Yousafzai was born on July 12, 1997, in Mingora, Pakistan. She is the youngest person to be awarded the Nobel Peace Prize, an honor bestowed on her at the age of seventeen. She is most well-known for her activism in support of female education and equality, which is an especially hot-button issue within her native country, a predominantly Muslim nation that has struggled for decades with militants and extremists (such as the Taliban in Malala's home province).

Malala grew a reputation for promoting education among women when she was still just a young child herself. Through determination, humility, and persistence, she showed her community how strongly she believed that girls should have the right to go to school and pursue an education. Sadly, she was shot in 2012 by Taliban members on her way home from class when she was fifteen years old. This attempted assassination was an attempt to silence her powerful voice for human rights—but instead of silencing Malala, her reach and influence only grew stronger and more widespread.

Because she was shot in the head and neck, Malala was left with some scarring and mild disfigurement on her face. Of course, Malala's belief in herself is demonstrated in many ways, and relates to far more than just her appearance. However, the following quote wonderfully captures what it means to have confidence in oneself and to believe in the power of one's own voice and vision: "My mother always told me, 'Hide your face—people are looking at you.' I would reply, 'It does not matter; I am also looking at them.'"

To this day, her bravery and quiet confidence continue to inspire millions of people around the world.

After all, as alike as we humans are to one another, each of us shares in the wonderful gift of our own originality and uniqueness. Perhaps it's our very differences, and our willingness to accept and celebrate these differences confidently, that will help bring us together.

So pat yourself on the back for picking up this book and let's get started!

Text-Dependent Questions

1. How could students benefit by being taught in leadership school?
2. What is the difference between confidence and cockiness?
3. What award did Malala Yousafzai receive?

Research Project

Write a one-page essay explaining the benefits of self-confidence in young people.

Words to Understand

confidence: a feeling of self-assurance that comes from a person's appreciation of his or her own abilities or qualities

flattery: excessive and insincere praise

Self-respect: a feeling that one is behaving with honor and dignity, or a view of oneself that is honorable and dignified

Social media users should be wary of becoming overreliant on flattery and, on the flip side, becoming targets of unpleasant criticism.

Chapter Two
LEARNING TO LIKE YOURSELF

In general, confident people like who they are. But how exactly does one learn to like oneself in the first place? Can *anyone* be self-confident and self-accepting? Are these traits that a person is simply born with, or are they personal qualities that can be developed?

As it turns out, psychologists and researchers tend to believe the latter. As a character trait, **confidence** and self-acceptance can be built, cultivated, and developed over time (no matter how many "successes" or "failures" a person experiences along the way). Just as a young person likes his friends, he can actually like himself, too, which tends to positively change the way he talks to, thinks about, and treats himself.

Self-Acceptance 101: The Dos & Don'ts of Liking Yourself

How does someone learn to like themselves more? Consider the following dos and don'ts:

DON'T Become Overly Reliant on Flattery or Criticism

It's hard not to, but young people shouldn't obsess over how many likes or follows they get on their social media accounts. It's not worth staying up all night worrying about what someone said. Remember that the negative things people say about others are really a reflection on the person *making* the comments, not the person who the comments are about. People who like themselves treat others kindly because they treat *themselves* kindly. People who don't like themselves tend to want to make others feel as bad as they feel, so they may gossip or say hurtful things.

It's also not wise to become too prideful when something good happens, or when someone says

A Thousand Roses vs. One Thorn?

Research shows that people tend to remember negative comments much more strongly than positive ones, even if they receive many more compliments than criticisms. Scientists believe that this is because negative emotions tend to require more thinking; our brains spend more time and energy processing negative information. So if you find yourself hung up on a mean thing someone said to you (even if you received ten times as many compliments that very same day), know that this is human nature. Awareness is key for change!

We will all encounter some criticism throughout our lives. However, rather than be upset by it, use it as an opportunity to reflect and learn.

something nice. Why? Because this can make someone forget about all the other people and circumstances that helped them achieve their success in the first place. Nobody truly goes it alone, and everyone gets help along the way. Plus, being too self-absorbed or stuck-up is a major turn-off for most people, and can make a person seem less trustworthy or likable as a leader.

In this way, the first step to liking oneself is to acknowledge but not depend on **flattery** or criticism. It's perfectly okay to enjoy compliments, and it's understandable to be hurt by insults. The challenge is to acknowledge these feelings and then as soon as possible move on and shift one's focus from the outside to the inside. What a person does and how they act are more important than what others think.

DON'T Beat Yourself Up for Your Mistakes

Everyone makes mistakes. These errors, whether large or small, shouldn't be ignored, of course. Without recognizing and learning from mistakes a person may miss out on great opportunities, ranging from acceptance to college, a job offer, or even a meaningful and loving relationship.

The concept of learning from mistakes is discussed in greater detail later in this book. For now, it's helpful to remember that people who ultimately like themselves are able to look at a mistake they've made and realize that the mistake doesn't make them a bad person. A person who is confident in herself can say, "I did a bad thing," instead of, "I *am* bad."

People who like themselves can accept that they're not perfect (nobody really is). They allow themselves to feel negative emotions like disappointment or guilt,

You have a friend in you!

Random Acts of Kindness Are Good for Everyone!

Research shared by the nonprofit organization Random Acts of Kindness shows that doing kind things for others actually increases the level of oxytocin in the body. Oxytocin is a hormone that is involved in social bonding, love, and feeling good.

but let go of these emotions as soon as possible. Then they focus on the solutions to their problems, not the problems themselves.

DO Help Others

Research shows that if a person is in pain or suffering in some way, doing something kind or nice for others can actually make them feel better. In this way, doing meaningful work for the benefit of other people is not about being selfless. After all, it's perfectly okay for someone to care about themselves! Doing good for others *feels* good for everyone, both the receivers and the givers.

Instead of being selfless, doing charitable work is really about showing love for oneself *and* others. So one of the most effective and simple ways to start liking oneself more is to do something caring and kind for another person or community: volunteer at a shelter or food drive, practice a random act of kindness, pay a meaningful and thoughtful compliment, or give a helping hand to a friend or even a stranger in need.

DO Treat Yourself Like Your Own Best Friend

A great question for young people to ask themselves as they build their confidence would be: "How would I show my best friend how much I like him or her?" Whatever actions or words a person would use toward their dearest loved ones can also be applied to themselves, too.

Treating oneself like a best friend requires that a person treats himself or herself with respect. **Self-respect** includes the following behaviors or habits:

- Saying or thinking nice things about oneself
- Spending quality time doing things one loves and enjoys
- Taking care of one's health and well-being

- Spending time with supportive, kind, and inspiring people (and avoiding people who are frequently negative or who participate in potentially harmful or dangerous behaviors)
- Taking pride in one's accomplishments and achievements

Text-Dependent Questions

1. Which types of comments do we tend to remember more easily, positive ones or negative ones?
2. Which hormone increases in the body when you do something kind for someone else?
3. How can you treat yourself like your own best friend? Name at least two ways.

Research Project

Make yourself a "confidence folder." This could be an actual folder, or you could use a journal or even a word processing file on your computer. What to do: any time someone gives you a compliment or any time you do something you're proud of, jot it down and store it in your folder. Remember, research tends to show that we remember the "bad" comments and setbacks much more readily than we remember the "good" comments and achievements. Building your confidence folder is a private, yet powerful way to help you remember all the good you have in your life, especially in moments when you're feeling stressed or down. Give it a shot: after one month, you may be surprised at how many wonderful things have happened that you otherwise would have completely forgotten about!

Words to Understand

Conscientious: wishing to do what is right, especially to do one's work or duty well and thoroughly

empathetic: showing an ability to understand and share the feelings of another

Thoughtful: showing consideration for the needs of other people

Spending time with friends is a fun and rewarding experience. Research shows that good social bonds are also good for your emotional and physical health. Positive friendships should ranks as high as healthy eating and exercise as a necessary investment in your health.

Chapter Three
MAKING FRIENDS

One of the hallmarks of a great leader is the ability to influence and inspire other people. This means that a leader of any age or reach must be able to connect with others and form healthy social bonds. Of course, this doesn't mean a person has to be a social butterfly or super outgoing in order to lead. Even introverted or quiet people can be confident in who they are and make a positive impact on others around them.

No matter what a person's individual style and personality is, he or she can cultivate fulfilling friendships (and deserves them!). Interestingly, the character trait of confidence can help a person make more friends, and the reverse is true, too—having many friendships naturally leads to greater confidence in one's own abilities and increased self-worth.

Top Ten Tips for Making Friends & Staying Confident in Social Settings

For some people, making friends seems easy and effortless. But even for those who don't feel this way, there are a few things you can do to make socializing easier.

1. Be Conscientious, Generous & Thoughtful

It sounds simple because it is! Good friends are kind and helpful. They offer compliments, provide assistance, share, support, and express gratitude. They do the right thing for their friends, which can include everything from following through on their plans to standing up to bullies and gossipers.

Friendly people also practice random acts of kindness not only for their own friends but also for other peers, coworkers, and even strangers. So one of the easiest ways to make a new friend is to do something kind or pay someone a meaningful compliment.

2. Show an Interest

Friends tend to have common interests: they may like the same kind of music, television shows, clothing styles, and even hobbies or after-school activities. And while friends don't necessarily have to like all the same things, they should show a polite and supportive interest in each others' lives if they want to have a healthier bond.

Showing an interest in a friend's life and well-being includes things like:

- Asking questions about their fears, wishes, likes, dreams, or even simply about how their day went

Research shows that those with good friendships and social support are better able to cope with grief. Support a grieving friend by being physically present, listening to them, and showing empathy.

Introversion vs. Extroversion

Introverts tend to enjoy spending time alone and prefer engaging in small, intimate conversations; they often find social situations energy-draining. Conversely, extroverts enjoy and become energized by being the center of attention and being in large social groups. Both introverts and extroverts can develop and maintain deep, meaningful relationships and friendships. Likewise, *both* types of people can thrive in leadership roles! The key is to focus on the unique strengths that each personality type brings to the table. According to research shared by lawyer and author Susan Cain, as many as one-third to one-half of the American population are considered introverts. For more information, check out her 2012 book *Quiet: The Power of Introverts in a World That Can't Stop Talking.*

- Attending friends' plays, events, shows, presentations, games, etc.
- Sharing friends' successes and achievements with others

3. Practice Empathy

When a person is sad, afraid, hurt, frustrated, or feeling any other sort of challenging emotion, he or she often will turn to friends for support. Great friends show support for their loved ones by being **empathetic** and trying to see things from the other person's point of view.

Sometimes, it's appropriate for a friend to offer advice or guidance on what to do in a challenging situation, especially if they are asked to share their point of view. In other cases, a grieving or upset friend may simply be looking for a shoulder to lean on, or a healthy way to vent their frustrations. In this case, showing a person they have been heard by saying something like, "I hear what you're saying," or "I'm so sorry, that must be so frustrating," can go a long way.

Other empathetic responses a great friend can offer include: "I don't know what to say, but I'm here for you," "Just remember I love and care about you," or "How can I help?"

4. Use Positive Body Language

Smiling is the great equalizer. It's an interesting experiment to walk into any room and smile, then see how many people smile back! It makes sense, of course, that this simple, nonverbal communication can make it easier to develop friendships, since a smile instantly makes someone look more approachable and friendly.

Other types of positive body language include:

- Making eye contact
- Nodding the head
- Standing still (not fidgeting) with arms relaxed at one's sides
- Shaking hands or gently touching someone on the shoulder or arm

5. Practice Good Listening Skills

Communication is the heart of good friendship. People are naturally drawn to someone who listens to them intently and respectfully. Here are a few key factors to consider when trying to be a better listener:

- Don't interrupt
- Use positive body language while listening
- Ask clarifying questions
- Pay attention and really *listen* to the person: try not to think about other things or just wait for the next turn to speak

6. Respect Your Friends' Privacy

Great friends feel comfortable sharing intimate and private details about their lives

Need a Health Boost? Make a Friend!

Research shows that having meaningful friendships isn't just good for your social life; it can actually improve your overall quality of living, health, and mental well-being. Having friends has been shown to help people cope with trauma, improve their self-confidence, decrease stress, increase their sense of purpose and belonging, and potentially even extend their life!

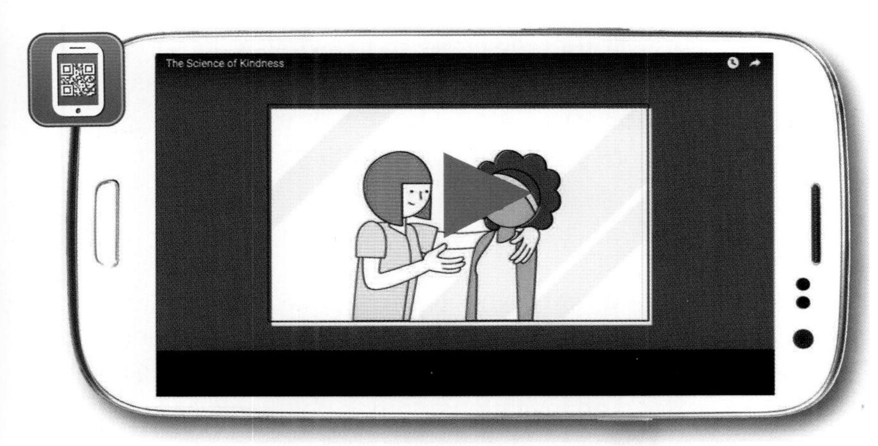

The science of kindness

These two girls are using body language to show their affection for each other. It feels good to interact with others in this way, and even adds to your own happiness.

because they can trust that their friend will keep a secret. In this way, a person can show that they're a good friend by not participating in unkind behaviors such as gossiping, snooping on a friend's phone or social media pages, or even demanding that their friends tell them more details about something than they're comfortable sharing.

7. Do Things Together

If a person wants to develop a closer bond with someone they know, simply spending quality time with that person will offer an opportunity to plant the seeds of friendship. And while it may feel a little intimidating to pick up the phone and call or text someone, it's usually better to extend an invitation and risk being told "no thanks," rather than never reaching out and missing out on a new friend.

8. Support Each Other in Healthy Behaviors

True friends would never pressure people into doing things they are not comfortable with. This includes risky or illegal behaviors such as underage drinking, unprotected sex, drug use, speeding, bullying, gossiping, shoplifting, cheating on exams, and so on.

Healthy friendships are ones in which two or more people can enjoy healthy activities together, like playing sports, cooking healthy foods, studying, and having challenging and loving conversations. Remember that to be a good friend, people need to do things together—but these things shouldn't be harmful or hurtful.

9. Resolve Conflict

Even best friends are likely to argue from time to time. A person doesn't have to simply agree with or like everything their friends do or say. If anything, true friends are willing to speak their mind and give honest feedback.

But when conflict does invariably arise, a true friend is able to acknowledge their role in the argument, do what needs to be done to correct the situation, and then apologize and move on. They pick their battles wisely and don't make a big deal out of little issues. Life is too short to hold onto grudges and resentment. Good friends understand that people make mistakes and miscommunicate sometimes; this doesn't necessarily mean the friendship has to be ruined.

10. Be Yourself

The final chapter in this book will discuss the ins and outs of what it means to "be yourself" in greater detail. For now, it's helpful to remember that, when making friends, a person should be able to feel comfortable sharing how they feel and think, doing what they enjoy, and expressing their own style and unique personality. If someone is being belittled or made fun of by their "friends," or being pressured to act in a way that goes against their nature, he or she may need to let that relationship go, which is a brave act of self-love that can build a great deal of confidence.

Ultimately, people want and deserve to be loved and accepted for who they are. By starting from within—by loving and accepting themselves—it becomes so much easier to love and accept other people for who they are, too, which is an incredibly attractive and appealing quality. Of course, self-acceptance is a lifelong practice that will have its ups and downs. But, for the sake of meaningful friendships, the practice is certainly worth it.

Text-Dependent Questions

1. What is the difference between an extrovert and an introvert?
2. Name two tips that can help you make new friends or feel more comfortable in social situations.
3. Are friendships good for your health? Why or why not?

Research Project

Become a "RAKtavist." Spend some time exploring the following website: https://www.randomactsofkindness.org. You can opt to sign up and pledge your commitment to becoming a Random Acts of Kindness activist, or simply read through the blog for inspiring ideas and examples of people helping others. After you've spent some time here, write a one- to two-page essay on some of your own ideas about how you can start spreading more kindness among your family, friends, school, community, and even the world itself. Enlist some of your friends and take kind and loving action together. You'll be surprised at how much it helps you form a closer bond with your loved ones!

Words to Understand

emotional: relating to a person's feelings

fulfillment: a feeling of happiness and satisfaction

self-esteem: a person's overall attitude about him or herself; how much someone appreciates and respects themselves

Most of us have some level of dissatisfaction with our bodies. This can be especially true during the teen years, when it can be made worse by bullying or unkindness from a peer group.

Chapter Four
BODY IMAGE

Body image, also known as "the way that someone perceives their body and assumes that others perceive them," according to the organization DoSomething.org, is heavily influenced by peers, the media, parents, and other factors. It can be healthy or unhealthy, and may change at different times in a person's life.

Young people (who are going through many physical, psychological, **emotional**, social, and mental changes) are especially prone to having struggles with their body image, but these struggles can happen at any age. In fact, research shows that a majority of both women *and* men in Western society are unhappy about the way they look.

A Quotation to Ponder

"Beauty is how you feel inside, and it reflects in your eyes. It is not something physical."

—Sophia Loren, Italian actress and singer

The Relationship Between Body Image, Self-Esteem & Confidence

Body image is a component of **self-esteem**. It concerns how someone thinks about their body, whereas self-esteem relates more to how a person thinks and feels about themselves overall. Understandably, if a person does not respect or appreciate themselves (e.g., if they have low self-confidence) they likely will feel badly about their body.

This may cause them to focus on their perceived flaws or faults, and compare the way they look to other people or images portrayed in the media. Not only is this frustrating and distressing to experience but it can also distract a person from achieving meaningful goals. Instead of focusing on what they would love to do and accomplish, people with low self-esteem and a poor body image often end up wasting a lot of their energy on worrying about what other people think and having negative thoughts about themselves.

Of course, it doesn't help that the media often show unrealistic and unhealthy "ideals" of what male and female bodies should look like. And in order for the youth leaders of today to promote a culture that focuses more on health and well-being than on looks and superficial beauty, they will need to learn how to feel comfortable about, and even celebrate, their own bodies.

In some instances, a teen can become extremely critical of their own body image. These concerns can constantly occupy his or her thoughts, leading to extreme disturbances in eating behavior. Those who experience this should seek urgent help from a trained therapist.

The Dangers of Low Self-Esteem

Research shows that having low self-esteem increases a person's risk for engaging in unsafe or unhealthy behaviors, including substance abuse and unsafe sex with multiple partners. People with low self-esteem are also more likely to stay in abusive relationships, tolerate unfair or harmful behavior from others, or even become perpetrators of abuse themselves.

Top Tips for Feeling More Confident With Your Body

All human bodies are impermanent: this means that bodies change, grow older, and eventually die. Instead of resisting this reality, or taking an excessive amount of pride in the way they look, confident and easy-going people are able to think about their bodies as gifts that should be appreciated and respected. Here are a few ways to do that:

Master Basic Health Habits
Practicing basic health habits on a consistent basis is one of the most effective ways to build and cultivate a positive body image and high self-esteem. After all, a person will have a much harder time feeling good about their body (and themselves) if they are not living in a healthy way.

The following are a few of the most important health tips to keep in mind:

- Eat mostly veggies, lean animal protein, and healthy fats, along with some fruit and whole grains.
- Avoid refined carbohydrates, junk food, and sugar as much as possible, but enjoy treats occasionally in moderation.
- Avoid harmful substances like alcohol, caffeine, nicotine, and illegal drugs.
- Drink lots water (a good prescription is around half a person's body weight in fluid ounces per day).
- Exercise daily.
- Practice meditation or mindfulness exercises.

Body Image

When is it poor body image and when is it a mental disorder?

- Get at least 7 to 9 hours of quality sleep (try to sleep in a pitch-black room and go to bed and wake up at the same time every day).
- If sexually active, practice safer sex by using contraception and getting regularly tested for sexually transmitted diseases (STDs).

Ditch the "Perfection" Myth

Those perfect images of men and women seen in magazine ads and on television commercials have been mostly airbrushed, photoshopped, and otherwise modified to portray the ideal of perfection. In reality, nobody's body is "perfect," and everyone has at least a few things about their body that they haven't figured out how to love yet. So it's a lifelong (and very worthwhile) challenge to accept one's so-called physical flaws. Understand that it's normal to be a little unhappy about certain physical traits, but that this doesn't have to ruin someone's life.

Confident people won't allow their day to be ruined by a pimple or some other blemish. Confident people don't spend too much time worrying about things they can't control, like the color of their skin, how tall they are, how many freckles they have, or how big their feet are. Instead, they acknowledge that their physical imperfections are most likely a bigger deal to them than to anyone else, and that it's just a matter of perspective. To help themselves adopt a more positive perspective, confident people focus their energy on things they can control (like how they fuel, move, and rest their bodies) rather than worrying about being or looking perfect.

Wear Clothes and Accessories You Feel Comfortable In

A person doesn't necessarily have to wear revealing or suggestive clothing in order to feel confident. Clothing is an expression of personal style and should reflect and celebrate a person's body type, as well as their unique personality.

A great idea from the business world is *dress for the job you want, not the job you have*. Attire, after all, has a powerful influence on the type of impression a person makes on others. To this end, a person can "fake it 'til they make it" by wearing clothes that send a message of confidence, maturity, and personal style.

Focus on What You Can Do & How You Feel Rather Than How Much You Weigh & What You Look Like

A great challenge for someone struggling with body image is to put down the mirror or smartphone camera, take a break from the selfies, and ditch the scale (at least

Learn to dress appropriately for every occasion. Wear clothes that feel comfortable and make you feel good. This will help boost your confidence. These teens are attending a prom night.

for a little while). Instead of obsessing over their appearance, people can learn to find confidence in their actions. Are they good friends? Are they developing skills in their extracurricular activities? Are they adopting healthier habits like exercising and eating nutritious foods?

There are so many ways to build confidence, and physical appearance is only one of them.

Consult With a Therapist or School Counsellor

Going to therapy and working through personal challenges with a licensed mental health professional can be an incredibly valuable and insightful experience. If someone is truly struggling with their body image or self-esteem, asking for and receiving help can mean the difference between **fulfillment** and failure—or even, in some extreme cases, life and death.

Try to adopt good eating habits by preparing healthy, unprocessed meals at home. You will then feel better about yourself and your body.

The fact is, everyone needs help from time to time, and it is not a sign of weakness to work with a therapist. The tools that people can receive and learn how to use thanks to the caring, objective, and attentive guidance from a trusted mentor or therapist have helped everyone from young teens to high-powered executives and world leaders.

And yes, even confident and self-loving people go to therapy!

The following websites may be helpful:
http://raisingchildren.net.au
https://adaa.org
http://www.apa.org
http://www.cpa.ca

Text-Dependent Questions

1. What are some of the negative consequences of low self-esteem?
2. List two or three basic healthy habits you can master that will help you feel better about your body and yourself overall.
3. What is body dysmorphia?

Research Project

Spend about 30 minutes researching body image issues among teenagers. Then, write a one- to two-page report summarizing what you've learned. You may want to include information such as: signs and symptoms of low self-esteem and poor body image, causes and risk factors for poor body image, and additional ways to improve it (in addition to those listed in this chapter).

Words to Understand

Conscious: having knowledge of something; aware

err: to make a mistake

shame: a painful feeling of humiliation or distress caused by the consciousness of wrong or foolish behavior

When learning something new, such as the complicated process of dressmaking, new students will only develop the new skills they need by trial and error. Invariably, it is only when something doesn't go right that we can learn how to get it right next time.

Chapter Five
LEARNING FROM YOUR MISTAKES

It's normal to **err** and make mistakes. Why then is it so painful and embarrassing to do so?

Many psychologists and other mental health experts rightly point out that it's not necessarily mistakes themselves that are the problem, but rather the judgment, blame, and **shame** people tend to place on themselves as a response to them.

It's actually been said that a mistake only stays "just a mistake" if the person who errs fails to learn something and grow from the experience. If anything, mistakes can be quite useful and important for people as they develop and grow, especially in the case of young teens and adults.

Three Tips to Help You Learn From Your Mistakes

Learning how to be grateful for mistakes and pay attention to the lessons they contain can help anyone gain confidence in virtually every area of life. Here are a few of the most helpful tips:

1. Take Time to Reflect on the Situation

Mistakes are often associated with heightened and intense emotions. If a

Learning From Your Mistakes

When you make a mistake, a common reaction is to get angry or sulk. This is a negative attitude to take. Instead, embrace the mistake for what it is, reflect on it, and take responsibility for it. Transform your error of judgment into a valuable life lesson.

Achieving Your Goals? Be Grateful for Your Past Mistakes

Scientific research has shown that making mistakes is actually an important part of learning. Brain activity (as measured with technology including functional magnetic resonance imaging, or fMRI) has been shown to increase in people who have recently made a mistake while learning new things, indicating that we are hardwired to process certain information more quickly and thoroughly so we can avoid repeating mistakes in the future.

person does not take the time to step away, breathe, and quietly reflect on an error, then their highly charged emotional state may completely prevent any learning from happening.

No matter where a mistake happens—in school, in a relationship, out on the sports field or stage—people who are even-tempered, confident, and insightful are able to regulate themselves by taking time to reflect on the situation. Which factors contributed to the outcome? What happened? Why? Is this a one-off mistake or a pattern that needs to be corrected? What could be done differently next time? Who can help? These and other questions transform a mere "error" into a valuable (if hard) life lesson.

2. Be Willing to Take 100 Percent Responsibility

If a person is unwilling to take responsibility for his or her actions and choices, as well as the outcomes of these actions and choices, then the potential for learning will be severely reduced. As mentioned earlier, confident and self-loving people are able to look at their mistakes from the point of view of "I'm only human" or "I'm learning" and not "I'm bad" or "I'm a failure." They will accept the consequences and do what is right, necessary, and fair in order to make amends, instead of looking for other people or things to blame for their setbacks. This shows both maturity and leadership.

3. Respect Your Process

Practice doesn't make perfect, practice makes *progress.* Learning new information and developing skills takes time, and it's important to allow oneself to go through

Learning From Your Mistakes

Learning is bravery

When learning a new skill, for example learning to drive, you are bound to make mistakes, and, at times, the whole process can feel quite daunting. However, once learned, skills such as driving become almost second nature.

this process naturally and patiently. Trying to rush or being impatient may only cause someone to make even more mistakes, thus delaying their learning and eventual success even further.

Decades of psychological research has actually shown four distinct stages of learning that most people go through at varying speeds. These stages include:

- **Unconscious Incompetence.** "I don't know that I don't know." This is the earliest stage, where a person is unable to do something and doesn't even realize they can't do it yet.
- **Conscious Incompetence.** "I know that I don't know how to do this yet." This is often the most difficult stage, when many people end up quitting due to self-judgment and frustration.
- **Conscious Competence.** "I know that I know how to do this." Easier than the previous stage, learners at this level still have to think consciously about the skill and it may still feel unnatural.
- **Unconscious Competence.** "I know how to do this and I don't have to think twice about it." The final stage of learning occurs when something is said to "come naturally" to someone. When riding a bike or driving a car, for instance, most people get to the point where they can do it easily without having to think about it. Depending on the topic or skill being learned (as well how diligently the person practices), this final stage can take months or even years to achieve.

People may move through these four stages at different rates compared to others, or even compared to themselves, while studying different topics; both genetics and the environment will influence the overall process. The important point, however, is to understand that in order to get to the stage

Top players, regardless of the sport, are successful because they have reached such a high level of unconscience competence. Their skills have become almost automatic.

of mastery and expertise, just about everyone must first go through the beginning stages—where mistakes are not only common but expected and welcome.

A Quotation to Ponder

"The master has failed more times than the beginner has even tried."

—Stephen McCranie, writer and illustrator

Text-Dependent Questions

1. According to popular philosophy and personal development research, when is a mistake no longer "just a mistake"?
2. Name two strategies you can use to help you learn from your mistakes.
3. What are the four stages of learning?

Research Project

Grab a journal and a pen and spend 20 to 30 minutes doing some self-reflection. Think back through your life and identify what you believe to have been some of your biggest mistakes, failures, or setbacks (try to think about mistakes in multiple areas of life, including school, relationships, sports, health, creativity, or even money). Now, write down some of the benefits of those mistakes: in other words, some good things that resulted from the so-called failures. Potential benefits could include lessons you've learned, new opportunities or relationships that came about because of the mistakes, or further challenges or obstacles you were able to avoid.

Words to Understand

criticism: the expression of disapproval of someone or something based on perceived faults or mistakes

emotion: a natural instinctive state of mind deriving from one's circumstances, mood, or relationships with others

self-talk: the act or practice of talking to oneself, either aloud or silently and mentally

When we are young our emotions are very unsettled. Have you ever seen a toddler crying one minute then laughing the next? As we get older our emotions become less erratic.

Chapter Six
DEALING WITH NEGATIVITY

Negativity, like positivity, is a part of life. The world has birth and death, creation and destruction, growth and decay, light and darkness. It's not really possible to have one without the other.

The same goes for emotions as well.

Emotions as Tools

Psychologically healthy human beings experience both "positive" (feel good) emotions and "negative" (feel bad) emotions. Emotions are often described as tools to help people pay attention and gain insight into their current experience; they can also be described as the physical expression of a person's thoughts (since we tend to "feel" our emotions in our body with sensations such as an increased heart rate, sweating, heaviness in the chest, or a "pit" in the stomach). The key is that both positive and negative emotions are normal and healthy.

To this end, it's not worthwhile to fight or resist one's own negative emotions. Instead, it's wiser to allow these feelings to be as they are, and to simply be more aware of them. An emotionally mature person can notice their feelings and emotions almost as if they were little children inside themselves throwing temper tantrums.

Once a person is able to become more aware of their feelings without letting the feelings completely take them over, they will be better able to let go of the **emotion** sooner and then move on.

In some instances, self-criticism can lead to chronic unhappiness and dissatisfaction with life. If you feel in need of help, speak to a school counsellor or therapist, who will help you focus on the constructive side of self-criticism and overcome your negativity.

How Many Emotions Are There?

2017 research from the Greater Good Science Center at the University of California, Berkeley, suggests that there are at least twenty-seven categories of emotions, ranging (on a gradient scale) from things like joy to amusement to envy. Some researchers believe, however, that human emotions can be boiled down to a few basic ones: anger/disgust, happiness, sadness, and fear/surprise.

Your outlook, your world

The Upside of the Downsides: A Few New Ways to Deal With Negativity in Life

Become More Aware of Negative Self-Talk

People tend to be much harder on themselves than they are on others. One of the most common methods of self-criticism is through negative **self-talk**.

The way that a person thinks is like a habit, which means that changing thought patterns can be difficult. One of the most critical first steps in dealing with negativity and preventing negative thoughts from hurting a person's self-confidence is to simply be more aware of these thoughts when they arise. Sometimes, it may even be helpful to jot down these thoughts so that they can be reflected on and broken down later.

Use Negative Self-Talk & Emotions as Cues to Pay Attention

Once a person becomes aware of how frequently they think or say negative comments about themselves, he or she can start learning how to use this awareness to help cultivate greater self-respect. How? By using the negative emotion as a cue.

To do this, it's helpful to think about a negative thought or feeling as a little light bulb or alarm turning on inside a person's mind, like a little automatic message saying, "Pay attention." That way, when a negative emotion or thought is felt, the person experiencing it can stop and ask him or herself, "What do I need to pay attention to about this situation right now? What is this emotion trying to tell me?" It can be extremely helpful to work with a therapist or school counsellor during this learning phase.

Dealing With Negativity

Pay Attention to Constructive Criticism, Not Cruel Criticism

Negativity is not only self-imposed, of course. Other people will often attempt to put someone down with hurtful comments or actions, too.

As mentioned earlier, people who feel badly about themselves will often try to make other people feel badly as well. The trick is to remember that what people do or say has more to do with their inner environment than with anything (or anyone) else. Very confident and mature people are able to ignore cruel comments and insults by remembering this.

Ignore unconstructive and cruel criticism. It is likely that those who attempt to make others feel bad have negativity issues of their own.

Throughout your school and working life you are likely to come across constructive criticism. This is usually about a piece of work or presentation you have made. This criticism, usually from an expert, is good criticism that will enable you to learn and progress to the next level.

A solid sense of self-confidence can also help a person identify when comments or **criticism** may actually have a seed of truth to them, which will allow the person to learn something and ultimately grow on a personal level.

Many philosophers and inspirational speakers note that it's impossible to have pleasure without pain, good without bad, or support without challenge. In a closed system ruled by the law of physics (like the known universe), things are always in balance, but it's human perspective and judgment that can make it hard to see that perfect balance.

For a happy, healthy life, accept the ups and downs you encounter on the way.

So learn to accept the good and the bad of life. Try to embrace the "flaws" as well as the "features." To live a full life, a person must be able to confidently and courageously deal with both the ups and the downs.

A Quotation to Ponder

"It is impossible to live without failing at something, unless you live so cautiously that you might as well not have lived at all—in which case, you fail by default."

—J. K. Rowling, British author of the *Harry Potter* series

Text-Dependent Questions

1. What is self-talk?
2. According to new research from scientists at the University of California, Berkeley, roughly how many different categories of human emotion are there?
3. Name one positive and effective way to deal with negativity.

Research Project

Spend 30 to 60 minutes researching Stoicism, then write a two- to three-page essay about what you've learned. Things to include can be some of the earliest founders of the philosophy, some of the basic Stoic beliefs, which public figures are championing Stoicism today, and how you can use Stoicism to help you combat negativity.

Words to Understand

authentic: genuine, true to oneself

hubris: excessive pride or self-confidence

self-determination: acting in accordance with one's true self

Be proud of your work if it is good. Pride can give a person a great sense of purpose and allows him or her to celebrate their small milestones of success along the way.

Chapter Seven
BEING YOURSELF

This entire book has been a series of insights, tools, and strategies to help the reader gain more confidence and ultimately achieve what this final chapter is all about:

The power and courage to be your **authentic** self.

Confident people adopt the belief that they can be, do, and have what they want. They aren't ashamed of either success or failure, and are willing to help others, to learn from their mistakes, and to be honest and humble. Of course, they feel all the same emotions that anyone else feels, including insecurity, doubt, and fear. But the truly mature and confident people of the world are able to stay in control of their emotions, instead of letting their emotions take the driver's seat.

At their core, confident men, women, and children are able to understand that they are inherently worthy as human beings. No matter what is going on in their life at the moment, they can be proud of who they are.

Is Pride a Bad Thing?

The word "pride" might bring up a few different ideas or images in the mind. On the one hand, pride in one's abilities can help someone remain focused and determined as they work toward a goal, such as studying in school or practicing their chosen sport or extracurricular activity. Pride can give a person a great sense of purpose and allows him or her to celebrate their small milestones of success along the way.

However, pride can become more of a negative trait when it starts to turn into **hubris**: for instance, when someone acts in a

Why Authenticity Matters

Psychological research points to the fact that being authentic (true to oneself) is closely correlated with a person's mental and emotional well-being. High **self-determination** (in other words, acting with authenticity and taking ownership of one's own life) is actually considered by some experts to be one of the basic psychological needs, and relates to everything from self-esteem to coping skills.

Showing respect for others begins with self-respect. Good leaders will genuinely care and treat others with respect, for they know that if they demostrate respect, they will be respected in return.

way that is cocky or self-centered, or acts as if they are more important than other people. Unfortunately, hubris can lead people to cheat, take advantage of other people, fail to learn from their mistakes, engage in violence, and do things that may harm others.

For this reason, it's important to make sure one can have pride but at the same time remain humble. Ultimately, the best and most likable leaders tend to like themselves, which allows them to take pride in their accomplishments while remaining humble and expressing gratitude to the things, people, and circumstances that helped them succeed.

The Top Dos & Don'ts of Being Who You Are

DON'T Always Just Do Things Because You Think You "Should," "Ought to," or "Have to"

Doing things out of a sense of obligation can lead to resentment and dissatisfaction. Confidence is a key trait that can prevent a person from giving in to peer pressure or doing things simply to impress other people.

DON'T Obsess Over What People Think

What others think about you is none of your business. This is a radical, yet powerful concept that can help a person release their concerns over what people may be thinking (and in reality, people are much more focused on themselves than they are about anyone else).

Being yourself: it's not rocket science

Being Yourself

DO Know Your Values

Family, culture, society, and individual factors all play a role in what matters to each individual, and so long as these values do not cause harm or take away the rights of someone else, people should be free to seek out and fulfill those values.

What are values? They include big-picture topics like honesty, integrity, family, wealth, and creativity, and also include smaller, more practical things and activities such as beauty, clothes, sports, reading, and so on. Confident people listen to their heart and recognize what matters to *them*, then live their lives according to those factors.

DO Pursue Your Goals

A great truth is hidden in Henry David Thoreau's words. The world needs the next generation of young leaders to be who they are and love who they are. Why? So that they will be better equipped to inspire and bring together others in their local and global communities.

Mahatma Gandhi is widely recognized as one of the twentieth century's greatest leaders. He gave Indians a new spirit, a sense of self-respect, and a feeling of pride.

Ultimately, it is confidence and belief in one's self and abilities, respect and patience for one's own self, and an easy-going and lighthearted approach to the drama of life that will help young people go far in school, work, relationships, and any other area. Self-confidence and self-love take courage and should be considered a lifelong practice, but taking the time to develop these qualities will allow young adults to enjoy and live their precious lives much more joyously.

A Quotation to Ponder

"Go confidently in the direction of your dreams. Live the life you've imagined."

—Henry David Thoreau, American essayist and philosopher

Text-Dependent Questions

1. How does authenticity relate to psychological well-being?
2. What does hubris mean?
3. List one do and one don't when it comes to being who you are.

Research Project

Write a list of the values in your life that truly matter to you. Doing so will allow you to understand who you are, celebrate your own interests, and help you achieve a more fulfilling and personally meaningful life. Be sure to highlight which values you've identified as your top priorities in life (e.g., reading, hanging out with friends, playing sports, etc.) as well as what, if anything, surprised you, challenged you, or inspired you.

Series Glossary of Key Terms

ability Power to do something.
addiction A strong and harmful need to regularly have something (such as a drug).
anxiety Fear or nervousness about what might happen.
argument An angry disagreement.
assumption Something accepted as true.
body language Movements or positions of the body that express a person's thoughts or feelings.
challenge A stimulating task or problem.
citizen A person who lives in a particular place.
clarify To make or become more easily understood.
collaborate To work with others.
conclusion Final decision reached by reasoning.
conflict A clashing disagreement (as between ideas or interests).
confusion Difficulty in understanding or in being able to tell one thing from a similar thing.
cooperation The act or process of working together to get something done.
counsellor A person who gives advice.
criticism The act of finding fault.
culture The habits, beliefs, and traditions of a particular people, place, or time.
discipline Strict training that corrects or strengthens.
discriminate To unfairly treat a person or group differently from other people or groups.
efficiency The ability to do something or produce something without waste.
effort Hard physical or mental work.
evidence A sign which shows that something exists or is true.
experience Skill or knowledge that you get by doing something.
feedback Helpful criticism given to someone to indicate what can be done to improve something.
frustration A feeling of anger or annoyance caused by being unable to do something.
goal Something that you are trying to do or achieve.
grammar The rules of how words are used in a language.
guarantee A promise that something will be or will happen as stated.
guilt A feeling of shame or regret as a result of bad conduct.
habit A settled tendency or usual manner of behavior.
human right A basic right that many societies believe every person should have.
humble Not thinking of yourself as better than other people.
innovation A new idea, method, or device.
inspiration Something that moves someone to act, create, or feel an emotion.

interact To talk or do things with other people.
intimidate To make timid or fearful.
judgment An opinion or decision that is based on careful thought.
manage To take care of and make decisions about (someone's time, money, etc.).
maturity The quality or state of being mature; especially full development.
media The system and organizations of communication through which information is spread to a large number of people.
memory The power or process of reproducing or recalling what has been learned and retained.
mindfulness The practice of maintaining a nonjudgmental state of heightened or complete awareness of one's thoughts, emotions, or experiences.
mind-numbing Very dull or boring.
motivation The condition of being eager to act or work.
nutrition The act or process of nourishing or being nourished.
opinion Belief stronger than impression and less strong than positive knowledge.
opportunity A favorable combination of circumstances, time, and place.
paper trail Documents (such as financial records) from which a person's actions may be traced or opinions learned.
perspective The ability to understand what is important and what isn't.
politics The art or science of government.
ponder To think about.
punctuation The act or practice of inserting standardized marks or signs in written matter to clarify the meaning.
realistic Ready to see things as they really are and to deal with them sensibly.
relationship The state of interaction between two or more people, groups, or countries.
resolution The final solving of a problem.
respect To consider worthy of high regard.
retirement Withdrawal of one's position or occupation or from active working life.
schedule A written or printed list of things and the times when they will be done.
setback A slowing of progress.
stress A state of mental tension and worry caused by problems in your life, work, etc.
therapist A person specializing in treating disorders or injuries of the body or mind, especially in ways that do not involve drugs and surgery.
trait A quality that makes one person or thing different from another.
trust To place confidence in someone or something.
valid Based on truth or fact.

Further Reading & Internet Resources

Further Reading

Brown, Brené. *Braving the Wilderness: The Quest for True Belonging and the Courage to Stand Alone.* New York: Random House, 2017.

Brown, Brené. *The Gifts of Imperfection: Let Go of Who You Think You're Supposed to Be and Embrace Who You Are.* Center City, MN: Hazelden, 2010.

Demartini, John. *The Values Factor: The Secret to Creating an Inspired & Fulfilling Life.* New York: Berkeley Publishing Group, 2013.

Schiraldi, Glenn. *The Self-Esteem Workbook.* 2nd edition. Oakland, CA: New Harbinger Publications, Inc., 2016.

Internet Resources

http://actualized.org This website is for "advanced personal development" and offers plenty of thought-provoking free videos covering a broad range of topics including confidence, happiness, productivity, and health.

https://tinybuddha.com A diverse and inspiring website sharing tons of inspirational, mindful, and self-loving concepts. Read articles and blog posts that can help you with everything from feeling more beautiful to letting go of negativity.

https://www.dove.com It's about a lot more than just soap on this company's website. Click on the Dove Self-Esteem Project page and find resources for teachers, youth leaders, and parents and mentors.

https://www.tonyrobbins.com/blog/ The blog of author and motivational speaker Tony Robbins is always a great read to explore when you're feeling as if you need a self-love or confidence boost. Learn about topics such as developing joyful habits, celebrating success, and putting yourself first.

Publisher's note:
The websites listed on this page were active at the time of publication. The publisher is not responsible for websites that have changed their addresses or discontinued operation since the date of publication. The publisher will review and update the website list upon each reprint.

Organizations to Contact

4-H: Positive Youth Development and Mentoring Organization
7100 Connecticut Avenue
Chevy Chase, MD 20815
Phone: 301-961-2800
Website: https://4-h.org

Annie E. Casey Foundation
701 St. Paul Street
Baltimore, MD 21202
Phone: 410-547-6600
Fax: 410-547-6624
Website: http://www.aecf.org

Boys and Girls Clubs of America
1275 Peachtree Street NE
Atlanta, GA 30309-3506
Phone: 404-487-5700
Website: https://www.bgca.org

Boys and Girls Clubs of Canada
400-2005 Sheppard Avenue East
Toronto, Ontario M2J 5B4
Phone: 905-477-7272
Fax: 416-640-5331
Website: https://www.bgccan.com/en/

Index

Picture Credits

All images in this book are in the public domain or have been supplied under license by © Shutterstock.com. The publisher credits the following image as follows: page 12: JStone, page 56: D-odin. © Dreamstime/page 6 above: Brianna Hunter, page 6 below: Rawpixelimages, page 7 above: Andrea de Martin, page 7 below Vladyslav Starozhylov. To the best knowledge of the publisher, all images not specifically credited are in the public domain. If any image has been inadvertently uncredited, please notify the publisher, so that credit can be given in future printings.

Video Credits

Page 17 The School of Life: http://x-qr.net/1Feh, page 25 Random Acts of Kindness: http://x-qr.net/1DJV, page 32 CrashCourse: http://x-qr.net/1EDj, page 40 TED Archive: http://x-qr.net/1GTA, page 47 FightMediocrity: http://x-qr.net/1Ft8, page 55 Big Think: http://x-qr.net/1EWo

About the Author

Sarah Smith is a freelance writer currently living and working in the Boston area. She is also a board-certified Doctor of Physical Therapy, licensed by the Commonwealth of Massachusetts. She attended Boston University, where she earned both her doctorate and, as an undergraduate, a bachelor of science in health studies.

Sarah has been writing for her entire life, and first became a published author at age fourteen, when she began contributing to a weekly column for her local newspaper. Since beginning her freelance writing career in earnest in 2014, Sarah has written over 1,500 articles and books. Her work covers a broad range of topics, including psychology and relationships, as well as physical and mental health.

Additionally, she has over fifteen years of professional experience working with typically developing and special-needs children, along with their families, in a variety of settings, including schools, pediatric hospitals, and youth-group fitness programs. She spent over thirteen years working as a private nanny and babysitter for families in both her hometown of Yarmouth, Maine, as well as in and around the great city of Boston. Sarah also has experience tutoring and leading teens and young adults as part of a variety of clinical internship programs for physical therapy.